I0880156

You Are My FAVORITE PERSON

You and I have favorites. Like favorite mugs and desserts and places to sit. Favorite colors and scents and seasons.

But I wanted you to know that
you're my favorite person.

It's easy to like you because
you are you. In a one-of-a-kind sort of way.
Just the perfect *you* sort of way.

#1

You brighten my world
by simply being who you are,
doing all the things that you do.

You bring out the best in every moment.
You make me smile and laugh.

And you know how to enjoy each other's company, sitting quietly side by side.

Through all of our plans and surprises,
no one else takes on life quite like you.

Days spent with you are richer and sweeter.

I love that we're connected in ways
only we understand. Like our favorite
inside jokes, the looks we give each other,
and the memories we share.

KLES
Rai
Spri

WORD RACING
CAMP ABC
Trivia
Trivia

Adventures with you are always worth having.
I love the ones we've already been on and the
ones that have yet to be.

When we're together, fears seem smaller,
and our dreams seem to grow.

You're my favorite person to talk to.
You listen with intent and share with kindness.

Even if we see things differently,
you accept me just as I am.

Being with you is equal parts meaningful and fun. And 100% wonderful.

I smile inside when I see you.
Even when you're doing everyday things.

Maybe even *especially* when.

I like that you know I'm better at some things
and that you're better at other things.

Your quirks are just as charming as your strengths.

You're the person I can count on.
And you show up for me again and again.

Wherever we go, whatever we do,
when I'm with you, I'm right where I want to be.

**I don't say this nearly enough,
but I think you're the best...**

...and like all my other favorites,
I'll pick you every time.

#1

COMPENDIUM.
live inspired

An imprint of the Crown Publishing Group
A division of Penguin Random House LLC
1745 Broadway, New York, NY 10019
live-inspired.com | penguinrandomhouse.com

ISBN: 978-1-970147-97-1

Writer: Miriam Hathaway
Illustrator: Liana Jegers
Editor: Kristin Eade
Art Director: Jessica Phoenix
Production Manager: Shannon Lery

2nd printing. Manufactured in China with soy inks on FSC®-Mix certified paper.

The authorized representative in the EU for product safety and compliance is Penguin Random House Ireland, Morrison Chambers, 32 Nassau Street, Dublin D02 YH68, Ireland, https://eu-contact.penguin.ie.